Who Was Andrew Jackson?

by Douglas Yacka

illustrated by Jake Murray

Penguin Workshop
An Imprint of Penguin Random House

For Dad and Francesco—DY

Dedicated to Harley and Iolene—JM

PENGUIN WORKSHOP
Penguin Young Readers Group
An Imprint of Penguin Random House LLC

Text copyright © 2017 by Douglas Yacka. Illustrations copyright © 2017 by Penguin Random House LLC. All rights reserved. Published by Penguin Workshop, an imprint of Penguin Random House LLC, 345 Hudson Street, New York, New York 10014. PENGUIN and PENGUIN WORKSHOP are trademarks of Penguin Books Ltd. WHO HQ & Design is a registered trademark of Penguin Random House LLC. Printed in the USA.

Library of Congress Cataloging-in-Publication Data is available.

ISBN 9780399539909 (paperback)   10 9 8 7 6 5 4 3 2 1
ISBN 9780399539923 (library binding)   10 9 8 7 6 5 4 3 2 1

Contents

Who Was Andrew Jackson?

It was still dark on the morning of January 8, 1815. In an army camp just outside of New Orleans, Louisiana, General Andrew Jackson sat alone in his tent. He had a very important decision to make. Andrew either had to surrender his American soldiers to the British army or lead his troops into battle.

Andrew left his tent and walked through the camp. He looked at the faces of the men who had fought beside him over the last few weeks. They were cold and hungry and tired. They had been fighting the British for weeks, even through Christmas and New Year's Day.

   To make matters worse, he and his men knew
that the British army was twice the size of theirs.
In every direction, the bright red coats of the
British soldiers surrounded them in the woods.

But Andrew had a plan. Even though his troops were outnumbered, they knew these woods better than the British. He knew that the British army wasn't expecting an early-morning attack.

And he knew that he wasn't going to return from the war as a failure.

Andrew woke his soldiers and told them to prepare for battle. As soon as it was light enough to see, General Jackson sent troops out in all directions, attacking the British from every side.

The British army was taken completely by surprise. They were not prepared for this type of battle. Many British officers and their general were killed quickly, leaving the soldiers without leaders to give them orders. Andrew and his men won a major victory in just thirty minutes!

The epic fight is called the Battle of New Orleans. Jackson became a national hero, and he was eventually elected the seventh president of the United States.

Statue of Andrew Jackson
in Jackson Square,
New Orleans

MAJOR GENERAL
ANDREW JACKSON

Throughout his life, Andrew would face difficulty and danger with bravery, just as he did on that morning in 1815. His actions helped to shape a young nation as it continued to grow. A self-taught man, he gave many Americans hope that they'd shape a better future for themselves. For this reason, Andrew Jackson became known as "the people's president."

Today, however, Andrew Jackson also is remembered for some shameful events, including his terrible treatment of Native Americans and for his terrible attitudes such as his support for slavery. Jackson was a very complicated man—stubborn, brave, quick-tempered, loyal, unforgiving—and he has left a mixed legacy for the history books.

The War of 1812

The War of 1812 was fought between the new United States and the British Empire twenty-nine years after America had won its independence. The United States declared war because the British were capturing American ships in the Atlantic Ocean and preventing trade with France. The British were also secretly assisting American Indian tribes. They were attacking American settlements that were expanding west and north into areas the British still controlled. The war lasted almost three years before a treaty was signed. The Battle of New Orleans was actually fought after the treaty, but the news had not reached New Orleans yet.

CHAPTER 1
A Brave Boy

Andrew Jackson was born in what was then known as the Carolinas on March 15, 1767.

His parents were from Scotland. They had come to America in 1765 in search of a better life.

Sailing across the Atlantic was a long and dangerous trip. It took around six weeks to cross the ocean in those days. Even after Andrew Sr., Elizabeth, and their two sons, Hugh and Robert,

finally landed at Philadelphia, their journey was not over. They still had to travel five hundred miles by carriage to reach the home of relatives in South Carolina. The area where they lived was called the Waxhaw settlement. There wasn't much there at that time, and most of the settlers were poor. In addition, the land was already home to Native Americans who had lived there for generations. They did not welcome these new intruders. Violence often broke out between the local Cherokee tribe and the settlers.

Andrew's father built a small log cabin for his growing family. He was a farmer who struggled to keep food on the table, and often worked seven days a week. It was a very hard life.

Andrew Jackson Sr. died in the winter of 1766, shortly before Andrew was born.

Now Andrew's mother had to struggle on by herself, with three boys and a farm to run. She was a very serious woman. She taught her sons about the importance of hard work.

As a child, Andrew was smart and curious. He learned to read at an early age. Most adults back then didn't know how. Andrew was also full of energy. He could be wild and defiant. When he played games with his friends, he hated to lose. He often fought with other boys, even those who were bigger and stronger. Once, when he was being teased, he shouted, "By God, if one of you laughs, I'll kill him!"

Until Andrew was nine, South Carolina was one of thirteen colonies belonging to Great Britain. But in 1776, the colonies declared their independence. War started— the American Revolution. The Jacksons supported the fight for independence. Andrew, still a young boy at the time, was chosen to read the Declaration of Independence out loud when a copy arrived in town. It was a great honor.

Andrew's oldest brother, Hugh, joined the American army and was killed in battle. Andrew was very upset and angry over Hugh's death. He and Robert wanted to be soldiers like Hugh. They wanted to fight the British and make them pay for the death of their brother.

But Andrew was only thirteen years old. When he tried to join the army, he was told that he was too young. The army made him a messenger instead. His job was to carry information back and forth between American army camps in South Carolina without the British army finding out. Andrew liked the adventure and danger, and was glad to help fight the enemy.

In addition to the British, Andrew had to avoid the Cherokee Indians, who were known as fierce fighters. The Cherokees had made peace treaties and trading deals with the British, and they were not about to lose them to the new American settlers.

During one battle with the British in Waxhaw, Andrew and Robert were both captured and taken to a prison in Camden, about forty miles away. The two boys were terrified.

From Colony to Country

Before the United States became a country, there were thirteen colonies in North America owned by Great Britain. Colonists had to follow laws made by the king of England. They also had to pay taxes to England for everyday items like sugar, paper, and tea. The people in the American colonies felt they were being treated unfairly. They began to protest. Eventually, a group of men met in Philadelphia to discuss separation from England. Thomas Jefferson, John Adams, and Benjamin Franklin were among this group. They declared the colonies' independence,

named George Washington as the commander of the newly created army, and the Revolutionary War began. It continued for eight long years. Many Americans lost their lives in the struggle for liberty. Finally, on September 3, 1783, the British signed the Treaty of Paris, which gave the colonies their independence. The United States of America was born.

A meeting of the First Continental Congress

One of the British officers ordered Andrew to clean his boots. That made Andrew furious.

He wasn't going to obey the enemy. Andrew gathered up all his courage, stood up, and refused! The soldier became so angry, he swung his sword at Andrew's head. The wound left a large scar that he had for the rest of his life.

Andrew and Robert were thrown into prison with very little food, water, or medicine. Many prisoners caught a serious disease called smallpox, including the two boys.

When the boys' mother found out that her sons had been captured, she traveled the forty miles to the prison. Elizabeth convinced the British to include her sons in a prisoner exchange, and they were freed.

Unfortunately, Robert was much sicker than Andrew. He died soon after arriving home. Andrew's mother also became ill and died a few months later. At only fourteen years old, Andrew was left alone.

Shortly before her death, Elizabeth told Andrew, "In this world you will have to make your own way."

Smallpox

One of the great dangers in colonial times was a disease called smallpox. It was easy to catch smallpox, so an epidemic could spread quickly through a town. Many children and adults died from this disease during Andrew's time. Fortunately, smallpox disappeared by the end of the twentieth century, so that today babies no longer need to be vaccinated to prevent it.

CHAPTER 2
Restless

In 1783, Great Britain surrendered. The Americans had won the War of Independence. A treaty was signed in Paris. It was a time of great celebration for the new country—the United States of America.

For Andrew it was not such a happy time. He had gone to live with his uncle Thomas Crawford. The two did not get along. Also, Andrew made trouble for himself. Once, he insulted a friend of his uncle's. Andrew told the man that he wasn't brave or strong and was only capable of killing a sheep. The man threatened to whip Andrew.

Andrew Jackson became known for getting into fights. His mother had always said to

"avoid quarrels as long as you can." But Andrew had a hard time controlling his temper. Especially when he felt he was being treated unfairly.

After his grandfather died in Scotland, Andrew came into some money. He had to travel to the city of Charleston, South Carolina, to collect it. Since Andrew was so unhappy living with his uncle, he decided to stay in Charleston, a bustling harbor city.

Andrew's inheritance was not very large, but it was more than enough to pay for food and lodging. Andrew was determined to take the extra money he had and turn it into a fortune. How was he going to do this? By gambling.

He began playing dice, which was a popular gambling game at the time. He also bet on horses. Unfortunately, Andrew was not very lucky. He soon gambled all of the money away. Even worse, he wound up owing money to many people.

At that time, it was a crime not to pay a debt. Andrew was in danger of going to jail for all of the money he owed. To solve the problem, he

decided to make one more bet. This was a very
risky move. He bet his only valuable possession,

his horse, on a game of dice. This time, luck was on his side. He won! Andrew used the winnings to pay off what he owed.

It seems that the danger of landing in jail changed Andrew. He tried to become more serious and decided to go back to school in Waxhaw. But he found that he didn't like it any more than he had as a child. So instead of being a student, he decided to become a teacher! People in town found it odd that he thought he could go from one to the other. In any case, Andrew soon discovered that he didn't like teaching, either. It seemed the classroom was just not the place for him. He was a young man now, but success was still far away.

In 1784, Andrew moved to Salisbury, North Carolina. He was now seventeen years old. Salisbury was a large town for the time. He hoped to find some opportunity there for himself. As it turned out, he did.

Andrew met an important lawyer in the town named Spruce McCay. McCay liked Andrew's confidence and allowed him to study with him. Andrew worked hard and learned quickly.

However, in his free time, Andrew once again found trouble. He and his friends spent their nights in taverns, playing practical jokes and gambling. Once, at a local bar, the young men threw the tables and chairs into the fireplace. Many years later, a woman from Salisbury heard that Jackson was running for president. She exclaimed, "If Andrew Jackson can be president, anybody can!"

CHAPTER 3
A New Frontier

Not all of Andrew's time in Salisbury was wasted. He continued to study the law and learn from McCay. Over the next few years, he grew more hardworking. At twenty years old, Andrew took the test to become a lawyer. He passed with flying colors. The only problem was that Salisbury already had too many lawyers. So once again, Andrew changed his course in life. This time he was ready for a big change. He decided to travel west to the rough and unknown frontier to seek his fortune.

The journey across the Allegheny Mountains along the Wilderness Road was long and dangerous. This area, located between North Carolina, Virginia, and Georgia, was the farthest west that the United States extended at the time.

The capital of the region was its largest town, Nashville. The vast area surrounding it would eventually become the state of Tennessee.

The land was rugged and wild. There were few rules to be followed. It was the perfect place for Andrew Jackson to put in use what he had learned in Salisbury. He planned to bring law and order to this territory. Besides settling the disputes among the settlers, this meant protecting them from the Native Americans in the region.

Settlers fought constantly with the Cherokee Indians. The settlers believed they were entitled to this land. But the Indians had lived there for generations, long before any white settlers arrived.

Cherokee village

The land did not belong to these newcomers. The two groups did not trust each other.

Jackson, like most Americans at the time, did not believe that Indians were equal to white people. Andrew did not understand or try to learn about the customs and way of life of these people. He considered them savages. He remembered attacks by the Cherokee Indians on the Waxhaw settlement when he was a boy. Now a grown man, Jackson joined a band of men to protect fellow settlers in Nashville.

Jackson set up an office to practice law in town. The people of the area saw that Andrew had talent. Soon, the governor of the area chose Jackson to become district attorney. His job was to put on trial anyone who might have broken the law. Jackson liked doing that. He devoted himself to serving the people of Nashville.

In court, Andrew couldn't always control

his temper. Once, an accused man stomped on Jackson's foot during a trial. Andrew swung back at him in an instant. His tough ways earned him the respect of the people. Andrew Jackson became a popular man in Nashville.

While living there, Andrew rented a room in the Donelson family's house. There he met their daughter Rachel. Rachel had been living in Kentucky with her husband. But it was an unhappy marriage. Her husband was a cruel man who became jealous if she even spoke to another man.

Rachel Donelson

So Rachel had returned home.

Andrew and Rachel liked each other right away and they soon became close friends. He admired

her courage and independence. Rachel was drawn to Andrew's determination and spirit. In time, the two fell in love and exchanged wedding vows in August of 1791. However, because she still had a husband, they had to wait three more years before their marriage became official.

Andrew and Rachel never had any children of their own, but they adopted Rachel's nephew and named him Andrew Jackson Jr. The couple adopted two more children and took care of several others over the years.

Throughout his life, Andrew's devotion to Rachel remained constant.

Andrew Jackson Jr.

CHAPTER 4
From Lawyer to Leader

Andrew Jackson became a success in Nashville. He saved enough money to buy a plantation just outside of Nashville. A plantation was a large farm. The Jacksons' was called the Hermitage. The fields of the Hermitage were planted mainly with cotton. Selling cotton made a lot of money, but growing it took a lot of work.

Like many other successful farmers in the
South, Jackson owned slaves. Living in small
quarters near the Hermitage, these black men
and women were forced to do the farming.
Life was horrible for slaves. As to how harsh a
master Andrew Jackson was, there is very little
information. After his death, one slave said she
had been shown kindness. He bought medicine
when needed and tried not to separate mothers
from their children. But for others, there were
public whippings—extra whippings of one

hundred lashes for slaves who escaped and then were recaptured.

Jackson was a businessman, and thought about slaves the same way he did the animals on his farm. He took care of them so that they stayed in good enough shape to work. As the Hermitage became more successful, he bought more slaves. At one point there were nearly 150 enslaved black men, women, and children on the plantation.

As a well-known lawyer and plantation owner, Jackson was now held in great respect. People called upon him to make decisions about local laws and disputes. Slowly, Andrew Jackson was being drawn into politics.

In 1796, Tennessee became a state. Like every other state, Tennessee had its own constitution—a group of laws about what was legal within the state. Andrew proudly joined the convention where Tennessee's constitution was written.

Federal versus State Laws

Did you know that in addition to the United States Constitution, each state has a constitution of its own? The founding fathers wanted to make sure that some laws were followed by everyone in the country. Those are federal laws. For example, it is illegal under federal law to kidnap a person. They also believed that individual states should be able to make other laws as long as they didn't contradict federal law. Today we still debate whether the federal government or the state governments get to make certain laws.

Statehood meant that Tennessee would now be represented in the US Congress. There would be two senators from Tennessee and one member in the House of Representatives. Andrew, now twenty-nine, hoped to be elected to the House. And he was.

Jackson's new job required traveling back and forth from Tennessee to the nation's capital. (At the time, the United States capital was Philadelphia, not Washington, DC.) It took more than forty days to make the journey by horse.

Andrew missed Rachel very much and Philadelphia was not to his liking. So he resigned from Congress after only a few months. Then, just a year later, friends convinced him to run for the US Senate. Once again, he won the election—

but once again, he resigned after only a year to be home with Rachel. Throughout his life, Andrew was torn between using his talents to serve his country and his desire for a peaceful life with his wife.

Instead of national politics, Andrew decided to run for office in Nashville as a state judge, and popular as ever, he won. As a judge, Jackson was tough but fair. He was still known for his fiery temper. Once, during a trial, a man with a knife and a gun threatened to kill Judge Jackson. The sheriff tried to arrest him, but he escaped from the courthouse. Andrew grabbed his own pistol and chased the man down. He shouted, "Surrender, you infernal villain, this very instant, or I'll blow you through." The man surrendered.

People respected his bravery and depended on him for protection. Jackson liked this. He had never forgotten the pride he felt helping the cause of the Revolution. He still wanted to serve his fellow citizens as a soldier. So in 1802, he decided to run for major general of the Tennessee militia. The militia was a small state army that reported to the US Army.

The man he ran against was named John Sevier. The result of the election was a tie. The governor of Tennessee broke the tie by appointing Jackson. From that moment on, Sevier and Jackson were enemies. It wasn't long before Jackson challenged Sevier

John Sevier

to a duel. On the day of the fight, however, friends managed to stop them before anyone got shot.

Another duel did not end so well. A man named Charles Dickinson insulted Rachel. Jackson insisted on a duel to defend her honor. Both men fired their pistols. Dickinson shot first. Jackson fired back and killed him. But Andrew had been seriously wounded. He was shot near his heart. The bullet did not kill him, but it remained there for the rest of his life.

Charles Dickinson

Rules of a Duel

In a duel, two people fought each other with certain weapons. In Jackson's time, gentlemen agreed to rules for a duel in advance. The goal of a duel was not usually to kill your opponent. It was to respond to an insult and uphold personal honor. This was called *satisfaction*. This is how a duel would happen: First, one man would challenge the other. Sometimes this would be done in a letter or even in a newspaper. If the challenged man apologized, then the matter was settled. If not, each man would choose a *second*. The two seconds helped set up the duel. They would agree on a time and place. The place was called the *field of honor*. Most duels were planned at dawn. Then, the type of weapon would be chosen. In Jackson's time, this would usually be a pistol. Lastly, it would be decided if the duel would be fought until one man was injured, or "to the death."

The duel would start with both men standing back-to-back, pointing their pistols up. They would then take a certain number of steps apart before turning and firing.

In many cases, the men would deliberately miss, or shoot their pistol into the air rather than at their opponent. This was done to achieve "satisfaction" without actually injuring the other or being injured. But many men were killed in duels as well. Today, duels are illegal.

CHAPTER 5
New Trouble with Old Enemies

Winning the Revolutionary War had not ended the United States' problems with the king of England. On the high seas, American ships were attacked by the British. Their cargo was stolen, and American soldiers were captured and forced to serve on British ships.

The British made trouble on land as well. They had convinced some Native American tribes to help them attack American settlers on the western and northern borders of the United States. The Indians did not like the British, but they hated the American settlers even more.

On June 18, 1812, the United States declared war on Great Britain. This was called the War of 1812.

As head of the Tennessee militia, Jackson was called upon to assist in his state and the surrounding areas. Andrew was eager to fight the British again. He still blamed them for the death of his brothers and mother. "The hour of national

vengeance is now at hand!" he told his men.

At one point, Andrew was ordered to bring his troops south to Natchez, Mississippi. The British were believed to be planning an attack on the neighboring state of Louisiana. Jackson's men boarded thirty boats and headed down the Cumberland River. But when they arrived, there was no sign of the British.

It was the middle of winter and the conditions for the soldiers were very harsh. The men waited and waited in the brutal cold. When new orders finally came, Jackson was furious. He was being told to dismiss the troops and send them all the way back to Tennessee. To make matters worse, the soldiers would have to march back.

Jackson wasn't about to abandon his men in their poor condition so far from home. He led the way five hundred miles from Natchez back to Nashville. He even used his own money to buy his

men food along the way. The men started calling him "Old Hickory" after hickory wood, which is very hard and almost impossible to break. The nickname stayed with him from then on.

The fighting was not over for General Jackson. In August of 1813, the Creek Indian tribe called the Red Sticks attacked a fort in Alabama. Around 250 settlers were killed.

Chief Red Eagle, leader of the Red Sticks, had sided with the British in the war. So Jackson was called to bring in his militia. This time, his soldiers got their chance to fight.

The Creeks were fierce fighters, but so was Jackson. While his men called him "Old Hickory," the Indians soon referred to him as "Sharp Knife." Many of Jackson's men died in battles with the Native Americans. However, many more Creeks were killed by the militia. In the Battle of Horseshoe Bend, over eight hundred Creeks died. After this, Chief Red Eagle surrendered, and the Creeks signed a treaty. The treaty gave over control of more than two million acres to the United States.

Chief Red Eagle

It might surprise you to learn that the man called Chief Red Eagle was named William Weatherford. Although his mother's side of the family was Native American, his father was Scottish. William was raised by the Creek Indians in Alabama. They gave the boy the name "Lamochattee," which means "Red Eagle."

When the War of 1812 began, Red Eagle and other Indian leaders agreed to help the British. The British promised in exchange that they could keep their land once the Americans were defeated.

Red Eagle led his tribesmen in the bloody Creek War. He was one of the few to escape the Battle of Horseshoe Bend. Red Eagle later surrendered in exchange for the safety of his people who had been captured. He helped to work out a peace treaty with the settlers. Jackson admired Lamochattee's courage and spared his life.

Yet, as hard as Andrew could be, he could also be kind. He rescued a Creek boy named Lyncoya, whose parents had been killed in the war. He brought Lyncoya back to the Hermitage. Andrew and Rachel adopted the boy and raised him from then on. In a letter to Rachel, Jackson wrote, "Tell Lyncoya I expect him to be a good boy." Lyncoya received the same education as Andrew Jr.

He lived at the Hermitage until he died from illness at only seventeen years old.

The US government was pleased with the job Jackson had done fighting the Creeks. He was promoted to Major General of the US Army. And now Andrew finally got to fight the British face-to-face. In the historic Battle of New Orleans, Jackson bravely led his troops to victory. It was a short but bloody battle. Nearly two thousand British soldiers were killed or missing. Amazingly, only eight of Jackson's men were killed.

By the beginning of 1815, the War of 1812 was over. The US

Congress presented Andrew with a medal of honor for his leadership. The people called him the greatest general since George Washington.

Andrew enjoyed the sudden fame that the war had brought him. Even so, he couldn't wait to get home to Rachel. For the next few years, his life was peaceful, with Jackson overseeing the plantation. Then in 1817, General Jackson was called to duty once again, this time by President James Monroe.

Andrew was needed in Florida. At the time, Florida was not yet a state. It was owned by Spain, but many Americans were

President James Monroe

beginning to settle in the area. The American government wanted to control Florida so that the United States would have a secure southern border.

The Spanish were not willing to give up Florida, but they did not have many troops there. Instead, much of the land was occupied by the Seminole Indian tribe, who the Spanish mostly left alone.

Seminole village in Florida

To protect their land, the tribe fought fiercely against General Jackson, but the war ended in defeat for the Seminoles. Spain sold Florida to the United States for $5 million. Jackson was appointed the military governor of the new state in 1821. No surprise, Andrew did not want to stay in Florida. As soon as he was able to, he returned home to Tennessee and Rachel.

CHAPTER 6
Road to the White House

Andrew returned to Nashville a hero. At fifty-four years old, he was ready to retire—he'd run the plantation and spend time with his family. The years of battle had taken a toll on his health, and his doctors advised him to rest. "I am truly weary of public life," he wrote to President James Monroe.

The Second Bank of the United States in Philadelphia

But Andrew's peaceful life at the Hermitage wouldn't last long. Jackson kept in touch with friends in Washington, and he didn't like what they were reporting. Politicians were making laws to help their wealthy friends. The national bank was making large loans to the northern states while neglecting western states like Tennessee.

It was unfair and it angered Andrew. He felt like ordinary citizens were being forgotten. He remembered what it was like to be poor. He worried that the US government was starting to treat citizens the same way the British had once treated the colonists. Laws were being passed that only helped the rich, and there were too many taxes that were hard on everyday Americans.

Jackson's friends tried to convince him to run for president. He was already popular with many Americans for being a war hero. People all across the country knew his name. Andrew said no at first, but in time he agreed. He was nominated for the election of 1824.

One of his rivals was named Henry Clay. The other was named John Quincy Adams

Henry Clay

Adams had gone to Harvard and came from an important family. His father, John Adams, had been the second president of the United States. Adams was the exact opposite of Jackson. Jackson grew up poor and had to work hard for everything he had.

John Quincy Adams

Election day arrived, and when the votes were counted, Andrew received the majority. Everyday citizens had clearly picked him as their favorite. Did this mean Andrew was elected president? No. Because the electoral votes had not been counted yet.

What happened next was wrong. Henry Clay agreed to give his electoral votes to John Quincy Adams. Why? For doing that, Adams promised to appoint Clay secretary of state. That was a very important job in the government.

With Clay's votes, Adams now had the majority. This deal became known as the "Corrupt Bargain." Adams was declared the new president. Andrew was furious. He believed in a fair fight, and thought the other side had cheated.

Soon after the election, Jackson and Adams were both at a party. Because of Jackson's reputation for dueling, everyone expected a fight. Instead, Jackson walked over to Adams to shake his hand. Jackson wasn't trying to make friends, but he was avoiding a fight. He offered Adams his left hand to shake, which was considered an insult.

Jackson did not give up his dream to be president. Soon after losing, he made up his mind to run again in 1828. Rachel begged him not to, but she could not sway her stubborn husband.

During all four years while Adams was president, his supporters and those of Andrew Jackson attacked each other over every political and personal reason.

It helped Andrew to have the support of some newspapers. At the time, newspapers were how almost all information was spread. People believed what they read, whether it was true or false. Jackson became allied with the owners of many powerful newspapers of the time so that he could create good publicity for himself and attack his enemies.

Both sides in the campaign of 1828 said nasty things about the other. President Adams's friends even insulted Rachel and spread awful rumors. They claimed that Andrew and Rachel were not really married, and that she was a woman not to be trusted.

Popular versus Electoral Votes

When US citizens vote, they are not actually electing the president. Instead, they are voting for a group of *electors* who will then vote for the next president. Confusing, right? The reason the founding fathers created the system was to make sure that states with a small population had enough of a say in the presidential election. The popular vote is the total number of votes, one per person. The electoral votes for each state equal the number of senators plus representatives in the US Congress. States with more people would have more electoral votes. But even small states would have at least three. Because of this system, it is possible to win the popular vote but lose the election. Still confused? You're not alone. Today, many people think we should simply choose the president based on who has the most popular votes.

Rachel had been sick for a while, and the stories spread about her made her condition even worse.

Jackson was infuriated, but he knew that arguing this subject publicly would only make things worse for Rachel. His love for his wife seemed to be the only thing that could stop his natural desire to get even. He vowed to a friend, however, that "the day of retribution and vengeance must come, when the guilty will meet with their just reward."

Some Jackson supporters decided on a smart tactic. They planned a big event to commemorate the Battle of New Orleans. It was to remind people of his great military victory. Jackson took a steamboat from his home and stopped all along the way to meet people and campaign.

He was more determined than ever to win. And this time he did! At sixty-one years old, Andrew Jackson defeated John Quincy Adams by a landslide and became the seventh president of the United States.

Sadly, he was not able to celebrate for long. Rachel died of a heart attack on December 22, 1828. She was also sixty-one years old. Jackson was devastated. He blamed himself for her death. Andrew buried Rachel at the Hermitage. He then began the journey to Washington to accept his new position. (It was now the nation's capital.)

The tomb of Rachel and later of Andrew Jackson as well

On March 4, 1829, Jackson was sworn in as the new president. In his acceptance speech, he declared himself grateful for the "free choice of the people."

Many of Jackson's supporters from all over the nation traveled to Washington. At that time, the White House was open to the public on inauguration day. Jackson was so popular that mobs of fans flooded inside. The party at the

White House became so wild that dishes were broken and rugs were stained. The inside of the house was nearly destroyed. Eventually, everyone had to be sent outside! It was not a dignified way to start Jackson's presidency.

The Big Cheese

Late in his presidency, Andrew was presented with a most unusual gift. A dairy farmer named Thomas S. Meacham gave Andrew a wheel of cheese. Not just any cheese, though. This gigantic wheel

weighed 1,400 pounds! The cheese was made from the milk of 150 cows. Jackson kept his gift for two years before it was eaten. It was served at a big party at the White House, where ten thousand guests devoured it in two hours. The White House is said to have smelled like cheese for weeks afterward.

CHAPTER 7
The Trail of Tears

Jackson had many challenges facing him as the new president. The United States was growing quickly in both population and size. Between 1800 and 1830, the number of citizens increased from over five million to more than twelve million. People wanted land for themselves and their families and were pushing the borders of the country farther west in search of a place to settle.

There were over sixty thousand Native Americans living in the Southeast. Many of them were Cherokee. Seminoles, Creeks, and other tribes lived there as well. The Indians of this area were peaceful, and not a threat to the Americans. They were traders and farmers.

Even so, white Americans felt that they had the right to own this land. Jackson agreed. He still saw the Indians as a danger to the young country.

Soon after Jackson took office, an area that had been established for the Cherokee people was

The United States in 1830

taken over by the state of Georgia. The Supreme Court said that this was illegal. And indeed it was. However, Jackson decided to allow it anyway. On May 28, 1830, he signed the Indian Removal Act.

It ordered the Indians to leave their homes and move to an area west of the Mississippi River. This area eventually became the state of Oklahoma.

Some members of Congress criticized this harsh new law. They said that it was cruel and unfair. Andrew argued that he was making peace by separating the Indians and the white settlers. He believed that he was creating a new state for the Indian people.

Over the next few years, nearly seventeen thousand Cherokee were forced to leave their homes and belongings and travel 1,200 miles to the new territory. The route they traveled became known as the Trail of Tears. Some were packed into crowded trains. Many others were forced to

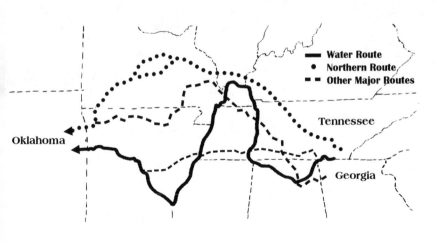

march. Thousands died of disease and starvation. Nearly one out of every three of these Indians did not survive.

To this day, the Trail of Tears is considered one

of the worst moments in American history. It is shameful that Andrew Jackson made it happen. It also became one of the main things that Jackson would be remembered for.

CHAPTER 8
Behind the Scenes

Even as president, Andrew Jackson still considered himself a man of the people. Many even called him "the people's president." Although he had been a congressman and a senator, he still did not trust politicians. He also had enemies in the government who supported former president John Quincy Adams. These enemies included John C. Calhoun, the man who happened to be Jackson's vice president.

Andrew wanted to

John C. Calhoun

change things in Washington. He believed that many people in government jobs were corrupt and had held their positions too long. He decided to replace some of them with men he trusted. Other jobs were awarded to people who had supported him during his campaign. This became known as the "spoils system." It was no better than the way things had been before and was actually just as corrupt. Jobs still were granted as favors and paybacks. The only difference was that Jackson's appointees were not the wealthy and elite people of Washington whom he despised.

Every president has a cabinet, a group chosen to look after different areas of the government. Cabinet members are called secretaries. Jackson, however, relied much more heavily on the advice of his friends instead of his cabinet. This circle of unofficial advisors became known as the "Kitchen Cabinet." It made Andrew even more unpopular with Washington politicians.

Free and slave states in 1830

At the time, one of the biggest questions was how much power to give individual states. Did the federal government have the right to tell them what to do? Many states, especially in the South, did not want a powerful federal government. They were afraid laws would be passed that they were against. Most of all, Southern states feared that slavery would be ended everywhere in the country.

Jackson believed strongly in holding the states together. He felt that if the federal and state governments were opposed to each other, the country would eventually fall apart. "Our federal union: It must be preserved!" he once declared.

At one point, South Carolina threatened to separate from the rest of the country. It was over a tax put on foreign goods that favored businesses in the Northern states. States like South Carolina had to pay higher prices for things bought from Europe in exchange for items Southerners sold, like cotton and tobacco. They called this the Tariff of Abominations. Vice President Calhoun was from South Carolina and supported his state instead of the president. He and Jackson argued, and Calhoun resigned in protest.

Jackson had always been stubborn, but he was also smart. There was no way he wanted South

Carolina to leave the Union. So he accepted a compromise suggested by his old rival Henry Clay. The tariff would be lowered. In exchange, the president would now have the power to use the army to force states to obey national laws.

This compromise was very smart on Jackson's part. Besides being able to carry out laws that he was for, Jackson also had the power to prevent Congress from passing some laws that he wasn't for. As president, he could do this through something called a *veto*. A presidential veto prevents a bill passed by Congress from becoming law. Congress has the power to overturn a presidential veto, but it is difficult to do. Jackson wasn't afraid to veto a bill he disagreed with. In fact, Jackson vetoed more potential laws than all six presidents before him put together!

CHAPTER 9
Battling the Banks

Jackson remained unpopular with politicians. But he was still loved by many ordinary people. He was nominated to run for a second term as president in 1832. This time his opponent was Senator Clay. Andrew won by a landslide.

Andrew continued to award friends with government jobs. One of Andrew's friends was

named Martin Van Buren. Jackson had wanted him to be the US Minister to England. It was an important position. But the Senate had to approve his choice.

Martin Van Buren

And they refused. Jackson shouted, "By the Eternal! I'll smash them!" In the end, Andrew got even. A president could choose his vice president. He didn't need Senate approval. So whom did Andrew choose? He replaced his former vice president, John C. Calhoun, with Martin Van Buren. Andrew Jackson had not lost his fighting spirit.

In 1835, however, he nearly lost his life. An out-of-work house painter named Richard Lawrence approached Jackson outside of the Capitol building. When Lawrence got close enough, he pulled out two pistols. Both pistols misfired.

Jackson then beat the man with his walking cane until guards arrested him. It was the first time anyone had attempted to assassinate a US president.

One of the biggest issues during the election had been the Bank of the United States. At the time, there was one central bank for the whole country. This system benefited the rich over the poor. Jackson believed that ordinary people should have banks in their own communities. He ordered that money from the national bank be moved to these smaller banks. Many congressmen were angry because of this. They voted to censure, or officially disagree, with Andrew. Jackson didn't care. He felt that the economy of the United States was in danger. It was his job to take care of it.

Jackson's personal experience had taught him to avoid owing people money, and the United States owed a lot to European countries. In 1835,

Andrew was able to pay off all of it. It was the only time in history that the United States has been completely debt-free.

In addition to paying back debts, Jackson forced France to pay back money that it owed. He made trade agreements with Spain, Russia, and Turkey. He even increased trade with his old enemy Great Britain.

But despite these successes, hard times lay ahead. Two years later, the country was on the verge of a depression. Over the next seven years, many people lost their jobs, homes, and savings. Some blamed this on Jackson's changes to the country's banking system.

By 1837, all of the states in the North had ended slavery. Most Northerners agreed that it was wrong. No person had the right to own another. Voices began calling for change from Congress. This was called the abolitionist movement. Most of the South disagreed. Their economy depended on slavery. Jackson, as a farmer with many slaves, sided with the South. He never saw slavery for the evil that it was.

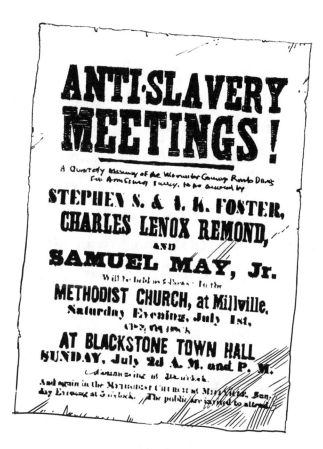

CHAPTER 10
The Last Years

His second term as president was over. He could have run again. But Jackson chose to retire to the Hermitage. He was nearly seventy years old. He was very happy to return home. But even there he did not rest. He eagerly went back to managing the plantation.

Andrew remained in touch with his friends in Washington. He had supported the election of President Van Buren. Many people still asked Jackson for his political advice.

Jackson continued to speak out against the corruption of the banks. He continued to criticize the wealthy for forgetting about the poor and only tending to their own interests.

But Andrew's body was not as strong as his

Presidential Terms

When the founding fathers wrote the Constitution, they did not set a limit for how many four-year terms a president could serve. Most of our early presidents, like George Washington and Thomas Jefferson, served two terms. They believed this was long enough and worried that serving longer made the president more like a king. The only president to serve more than two terms was Franklin D. Roosevelt, who was elected four times. In 1951, an amendment was added to the Constitution that limits presidents to two elected terms.

Franklin D. Roosevelt

mind anymore. The bullet in his chest from that long-ago duel caused him a lot of pain. He developed a lung disease called tuberculosis. On June 8, 1845, Andrew Jackson died, surrounded by his family. He was buried at the Hermitage next to his beloved Rachel.

Andrew Jackson was a man of his time, not ahead of his time like such leaders as Abraham Lincoln, who abolished slavery, or Franklin D. Roosevelt, who got the country through the Great Depression and World War II.

Andrew Jackson represented some of the best and worst qualities of Americans in the early 1800s. He was brave and confident, someone who fought for what he believed in. Although a poor boy with little education, he was able to become president of the United States. Yet he was a man with many prejudices. He believed white people were naturally better than others. He had no respect for Native Americans.

Andrew on Broadway

In 2010, Andrew Jackson got his chance to star on Broadway! A rock musical called *Bloody Bloody Andrew Jackson* opened at the Bernard B. Jacobs Theatre. It followed Jackson's life and presidency as if he had been a rock star. Songs included "Ten Little Indians" and "The Corrupt Bargain." The show cost $4.5 million to produce. Most critics liked it, but it closed after only three and a half months. The real Andrew Jackson probably couldn't have imagined this.

Although he believed in giving ordinary people a fair chance at a good life, he did not think Native Americans were entitled to the same opportunities, and he took away their homes and land. He did not understand why slavery was wrong, and owned more than 150 slaves himself.

In 1928, Andrew Jackson was honored by having his portrait on the front of the twenty-dollar bill.

Then in 2016, the US Treasury Department announced it would remove Andrew Jackson

Harriet Tubman

from the front of the twenty-dollar bill. Who was to take his place? Harriet Tubman, a black woman who had been a slave and who helped hundreds of other slaves escape north to freedom.

Timeline of Andrew Jackson's Life

1767	Born March 15 in the Waxhaw settlement
1780	Becomes a courier for the American militia
1781	Mother and brother die
1787	Becomes a lawyer
1791	Marries Rachel
1796	Elected to US House of Representatives for Tennessee
1797	Elected to the US Senate for Tennessee
1798	Becomes a state judge
1802	Appointed major general of the state militia
1806	Kills Charles Dickinson in a duel
1809	Adopts Andrew Jackson Jr. with Rachel
1814	Victory at the Battle of Horseshoe Bend
1815	Defeats the British at the Battle of New Orleans
1821	Appointed provisional governor of Florida
1824	Runs for president, loses to John Quincy Adams
1828	Elected president of the United States
	Rachel dies
1830	Signs the Indian Removal Act
1832	Reelected president for a second term
1835	Pays off national debt
1845	Dies on June 8 at the Hermitage

Timeline of the World

1773	Boston Tea Party
1776	The Declaration of Independence is signed
1783	First steamboat is built
	The War for Independence is won
1789	The French Revolution begins
1791	The First Bank of the United States is established
1796	The Southwest Territory becomes the state of Tennessee
1800	US capital moved from Philadelphia to Washington, DC
1804	World population reaches one billion
1808	Beethoven performs his Fifth Symphony
1809	Abraham Lincoln is born
1819	Spain sells Florida to the United States
1820	Antarctica is discovered
1828	Construction begins on the Baltimore and Ohio Railroad
1832	City of Jacksonville, Florida, incorporated
1836	Battle of the Alamo in Texas
1837	Queen Victoria of England is crowned
1848	California gold rush begins

Bibliography

* Books for young readers

* Behrman, Carol H. *Andrew Jackson.* Minneapolis: Lerner Publishing Group, 2005.

Brands, H. W. *Andrew Jackson: His Life and Times*. New York: Doubleday, 2006.

Meacham, Jon. *American Lion: Andrew Jackson in the White House*. New York: Random House, 2008.

Remini, Robert V. *Andrew Jackson: A Biography*. New York: St. Martin's Press, 2009.

* Yomtov, Nel. *Andrew Jackson: Heroic Leader or Cold-Hearted Ruler?* North Mankato, MN: Capstone Press, 2014.

Websites

American History: From Revolution to Reconstruction and Beyond:

    University of Groningen

    www.let.rug.nl/usa

Andrew Jackson's Hermitage: Home of The People's President

    www.thehermitage.com

The White House: Presidents

    https://www.whitehouse.gov/1600/Presidents